Science Vocabulary Quick Starts

Author: Linda Armstrong
Editor: Mary Dieterich
Proofreaders: Margaret Brown and Cindy Neisen

COPYRIGHT © 2018 Mark Twain Media, Inc.

ISBN 978-1-62223-695-4

Printing No. CD-405018

Mark Twain Media, Inc., Publishers
Distributed by Carson-Dellosa Publishing LLC

Table of Contents

Introduction to the Teacher

Science Vocabulary Quick Starts help students review science terms they have previously learned so they can retain the information and learn to use the terms in the classroom and in real life. The activities provide students with a quick start for the day's lesson by focusing on a few terms from a topic of study.

The quick starts activities in this book include matching, fill-in, true-false, word scrambles, and other activities to help students build and maintain a powerful science vocabulary. Each page contains two to four quick starts.

Suggestions for using *Science Vocabulary Quick Starts* activities include:

- Copy and cut apart the quick starts on each page. Give students one activity each day at the beginning of class.
- Give each student a copy of the entire page to keep in their binders and complete as assigned.
- Make transparencies of individual quick starts and complete or correct the activities as a group.
- Put copies of quick starts in a learning center for students to complete on their own.
- Use as homework assignments.
- Use quick starts as questions for a review game such as a science bee.
- Use quick starts as a quick activity before dismissal.

Ideas for reviewing and expanding science vocabulary include:

- Play hangman using science words.
- Generate crossword puzzles online for centers, homework, or extra credit.
- Generate word searches with clues online.
- Host frequent class discussions of science topics using correct terminology.
- Encourage students to use accurate scientific vocabulary to state and defend their explanations and observations.
- Encourage students to read about science. Excellent up-to-date materials are available from the library or online.
- Review Greek and Latin word roots.
- Emphasize the importance of precise terminology when writing about topics in mathematics and science.

General Science Vocabulary

General Science 1

Fill in the missing letters.

1. small piece

   p __ r __ __ c __ __

2. way of working

   me __ __ o __

3. knowledge

   __ c __ __ __ c __

4. grow larger

   __ xp __ __ __

5. get smaller

   c __ __ t __ a __ __

General Science 2

Use the clues to unscramble these words.

1. an idea proven to be true:

   ctaf _____

2. a group of organized, related things:

   emysst _____

3. something that makes something else happen:

   seuca _____

4. something that has been made to happen:

   ctffee _____

General Science 3

Draw lines to match the words with their meanings.

1. concept   write down or save

2. observe   find similarities

3. compare   find differences

4. contrast   idea

5. record   watch

General Science 4

Fill in the missing letters.

1. a final decision, answer, or ending

   c __ __ c __ __ s __ __ n

2. facts, ideas, or information

   __ __ t __

3. gather together

   c __ __ __ e __ t

4. studying the parts of a whole

   __ n __ l __ s __ __

5. an ordered way of thinking

   l __ __ i __

General Science Vocabulary

General Science 5

Fill in the blank with the correct word from the box.

> repeat   experiment
> identify   theory
> hypothesis

1. a logical, testable explanation _____
2. an explanation made as a starting place for discussion _____
3. a controlled test made to gain knowledge _____
4. to define or name something _____
5. to do or say again _____

General Science 6

Circle the best meaning for each word.

1. term: word   bird   rock
2. grid: oil   time   mesh
3. simple: old   basic   belief
4. complex: complicated   easy   fast
5. compound: flat   combination   single

General Science 7

Read each clue. Unscramble the word.

1. to research: **iesntigatev** _____
2. a skilled way of working: **uechteqni** _____
3. to define size, weight, or temperature: **sureame** _____
4. a state of being, such as sickness or health:
   itioncodn _____
5. something that has mass and occupies space:
   ansustceb _____

General Science Vocabulary

General Science 8

Draw lines to match words with meanings.

1. state   basic

2. force   move

3. fundamental   temporary form

4. flow   part

5. unit   energy

General Science 9

Write the best word on each line.

phenomenon, supplemental, finite, infinite

1. _____ means limited.

2. _____ means without limits.

3. _____ means additional or extra.

4. A _____ is something you experience with your senses.

General Science 10

Write T for true or F for false.

____ 1. A *category* is a kind of panther.

____ 2. The word *rapid* means very fast.

____ 3. To *combine* means to take apart.

____ 4. If something is *toxic*, it is poisonous.

____ 5. To *penetrate* means to measure.

General Science 11

Circle the best meaning for each word.

1. device: animal   cloud   instrument

2. occur: expand   happen   observe

3. abundant: plentiful   rare   interesting

4. origin: part   chain   beginning

5. transform: expand   compare   change

General Science Vocabulary

General Science 12

Write the word from the box that matches each clue.

| volume | mass | weight |
| density | speed | |

1. mass per measured unit of an object; compactness _____
2. rate of motion; fast or slow _____
3. amount of matter an object contains _____
4. amount of space an object occupies _____
5. heaviness or lightness of an object _____

General Science 13

Circle True or False for each statement.

1. When a planet *rotates*, it turns on its axis.   True   False
2. A *component* is a kind of fish.   True   False
3. To *alternate* means to go back and forth.   True   False
4. A *cycle* is something that happens once and stops.   True   False

General Science 14

Draw lines to match each term to its meaning.

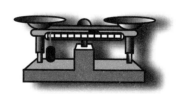

1. kilogram   a hundredth of a meter
2. gram   basic metric unit of weight
3. milligram   a thousandth of a meter
4. millimeter   a thousandth of a gram
5. centimeter   a thousand grams

General Science Vocabulary

General Science 15

Use each clue to unscramble the word.

1. heat or cold

   eureteratmp _____

2. metric temperature scale

   siCusel _____

3. unit of temperature measurement

   gdreee _____

4. temperature scale used in the U.S.A.

   hreFheanit _____

General Science 16

Use each clue to unscramble the word.

1. take in

   sobarb _____

2. equality

   lceanba _____

3. power to float

   uoycyban _____

4. a particular quality

   actticarerchsi _____

5. sort

   ssayifcl _____

General Science 17

Draw lines connecting clues to terms.

1. width   evaluate

2. most important   evidence

3. judge results   flow chart

4. data supporting   dominant
   a conclusion

5. diagram showing   diameter
   steps

General Science 18

Fill in the missing letters.

1. assigned duty

   f ___ ___ ct ___ ___ n

2. reasoning from something known

   ___ n ___ ___ r ___ ___ ___ e

3. inquire or examine

   in ___ ___ ___ ti ___ a ___ e

4. meters and kilograms

   m ___ ___ ___ ___ c measurements

5. description used for discussion and investigation

   m ___ d ___ l

General Science Vocabulary

General Science 19

Circle the clue that matches each word.

1. act of moving: dominance

    movement
2. object: thing

    phase
3. observing: noticing

    flowing
4. phase: evidence

    stage
5. predict: believe

    foretell

General Science 20

Fill in the missing letters.

1. The temperature in the special cooler remained

    c ___ n ___ ___ a ___ t.
2. The amount of salt added to the boiling water was the

    v ___ r ___ ___ ___ l ___

    in the experiment.
3. When a tree falls, its wood begins to d ___ ___ ___ y.
4. The a ___ ___ ___ ___ g ___ rainfall in our town is 40 inches per year.

General Science 21

Write the word that best completes each sentence.

**interference   equilibrium
imbalance**

1. Snowfall and melting reached an _____, and the glacier stopped growing.
2. An _____ in squirrel birth and death rates caused overpopulation.

General Science 22

Use the clues to unscramble the words
.

1. sensible:

    bsonaealer _____
2. measure:

    afyntiqu _____
3. become larger:

    crseeina _____
4. reaction:

    nesrpose _____

General Science Vocabulary

General Science 23

Write the correct term from the box on each line.

> property   purpose
> scientific explanations
> scientific procedures
> sequence

1. reason for existing

   _____

2. order _____

3. a distinctive quality _____

4. statements based on logic, observation, and testing

   _____

5. logical, orderly working methods _____

General Science 24

Write the word from the box that best completes each sentence.

> thriving   transfer
> variables   volume
> Venn diagram

1. He drew a _____ to show which animals ate both insects and seeds.

2. The _____ of the tank was 38 cubic meters.

3. The meadow was a _____ community of plants and animals.

4. Temperature, rainfall, and wind direction were important _____.

5. Genes _____ information from one generation to the next.

General Science Vocabulary

General Science 25

Write the word that best fits each clue.

stable, structure, system, technique

1. constant, maintaining form

   _____

2. the way tissues, organs, or rock layers are arranged

   _____

3. way of working

   _____

4. a group of objects or parts acting together

   _____

General Science 26

Circle the word that best fits each clue.

1. order: segment   sequence

2. outcome: cause   result

3. exact: precise   estimate

4. part: segment   system

5. identify: assume   name

General Science 27

Circle T for true or F for false.

1. *Efficiency* means the best use of energy. T F

2. To *assume* means to prove. T F

3. To *extend* means to stretch out. T F

4. To *belong* means to be left out. T F

5. To *conclude* means to observe. T F

General Science 28

Write the best word in each blank.

valid   series   test   study

In a recent year-long (1) _____, scientists ran a (2) _____ of experiments to (3) _____ Professor Kramer's hypothesis. They had to be sure that his explanation was (4) _____.

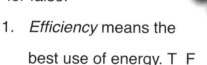

General Science Vocabulary

General Science 29

Fill in the missing letters.

1. a well-established observation about nature

   __ c __ e __ ti __ __ c l __ __

2. a preliminary idea about how something in nature works

   s __ __ __ n __ i __ ic m __ d __ l

3. a testable model based on repeatable experimental evidence

   s __ ien __ __ __ ic __ h __ o __ y

4. use of observation and experimentation to develop and test ideas

   s __ i __ n __ __ __ ic m __ __ __ od

5. information supporting or disproving a scientific idea

   __ __ __ __ __ __ ific e __ __ d __ n __ e

General Science 30

Write the best term on each line.

random	regulate
reject	cyclic
dehydrate	

1. You must _____ the temperature in an incubator.

2. Instead of picking particular eggs, we chose some at _____.

3. We had to _____ and discard two eggs.

4. We used warm air to _____ apricots.

5. Rainfall, runoff, and evaporation are part of a _____ process.

General Science Vocabulary

General Science 31

Draw a line to connect the word with its definition.

1. collide   does not change

2. absolute   depends upon

3. principles   changing

4. relative   conditions

                     run into each other

                     fundamental rules or laws

General Science 32

Circle T for true or F for false.

1. When water changes to ice, it is a reversible process. T F

2. Scientists never evaluate the results of their experiments. T F

3. If there is more food today, the quality of the food has increased. T F

4. If there is more pollution, the quantity of pollution has increased. T F

General Science 33

Use the clue to unscramble each word.

1. how often something happens: **uenfrcyeq** _____

2. how things depend on each other: **onsitterreinlahip** _____

3. likely: **babperol** _____

4. move away: **drecee** _____

5. move toward: **vacenad** _____

General Science 34

Draw a line to match each word with the best clue.

1. replicate   importance

2. submerge   nonliving

3. boundary   sink

4. inorganic   copy

5. significance   limit

Life Science Vocabulary

Life Science 1

Fill in the missing letters.

1. Sorting items into groups

   cl __ __ __ ifi __ __ t __ __ n

2. Things that are not alive.

   __ __ __ l __ __ __ __ g

3. Scientific term for things that are alive

   o __ g __ n __ __ __ s

4. Specific types of living things

   s __ __ c __ __ s

Life Science 2

Fill in the blanks with one of these words.

herbivores, carnivores, omnivores

1. Animals that eat only meat are

   _____.

2. Animals that eat only plants are

   _____.

3. Animals that eat meat and plants are

   _____.

Life Science 3

Circle T for true or F for false.

1. A food web includes producers, consumers, and decomposers. T F

2. A producer breaks down dead plants and animals. T F

3. A producer changes light energy to food energy. T F

4. Consumers eat producers. T F

5. A food web is a special spider web. T F

Life Science 4

Draw lines to match words to clues.

1. mammal
2. reptile
3. amphibian
4. bird
5. mollusk

a. is an invertebrate
b. lives part of life on land and part in water
c. has fur or hair
d. has scales
e. has feathers

Life Science Vocabulary

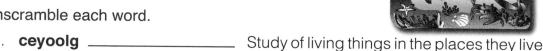

Life Science 5

Unscramble each word.

1. **ceyoolg** _____ Study of living things in the places they live
2. **mmncotiuy** _____ Group of living things
3. **eerhpoibs** _____ Area of the planet where organisms live
4. **eeonnnirmtv** _____ Air, water, or land around a living thing
5. **onaaatpdti** _____ Change that helps a living thing fit its surroundings

Life Science 6

Circle the word that fits each meaning.

1. coloration that hides an animal: diversity   camouflage   prey
2. an animal that is hunted: transpiration   camouflage   prey
3. the act of imitating or copying: mimicry   parasitism   osmosis
4. disappearing from the earth: osmosis   extinction   diversity
5. an animal that hunts: predator   gene   diversity

Life Science 7

Write the term from the box that best fits each clue.

pistil	petal
stigma	pollen
ovary	

1. base of the pistil, where seeds develop _____
2. sticky tip of the style, receives pollen _____
3. fertilizes ovules to create seeds _____
4. often colorful, helps to attract insects _____
5. the ovary, style, and stigma of a flower _____

Life Science Vocabulary

Life Science 8

Circle the best example for each term.

1. offspring:

    calf   rock   soil

2. trait:

    cat   ocean   eye color

3. behavior:

    size   diving   caves

4. habitat:

    chasing   howling   forest

5. juvenile:

    desert   kitten   markings

Life Science 9

Fill in the blank with the letter of the correct word.

A. life cycle   B. maturity
C. inheritance   D. lifespan

1. A certain beak, size, and coloring are a bird's _____.
2. The tadpole phase is part of a frog's _____.
3. The length of an animal's life is its _____.
4. A term for an animal's adulthood is _____.

Life Science 10

Draw lines to match terms and definitions

1. membrane   control center of a cell

2. cytoplasm   contents of a cell, except the nucleus

3. cell   tiny structures with special tasks

4. organelles   a basic unit of life

5. nucleus   a thin wall or layer

Life Science 11

Circle T for true or F for false.

1. Diversity means that only one type of animal lives in an area. T F
2. Genes carry the code of heredity. T F
3. Some animals survive the winter by hibernating. T F
4. Migration is a way for animals to hide from enemies. T F
5. A larva is an adult insect. T F

Life Science Vocabulary

Life Science 12

Circle the word or words in each line that are parts of a tree.

1. branch   crown

2. compost   bulb

3. cone   humus

4. needle   limb

Life Science 13

Write the letter of the best word on each line.

A. seeds, B. germinate, C. embryo, D. propagation, E. runners

Our class is studying plant (1) _____. We planted some (2) _____. Each seed contained a baby plant, or (3) _____. It took a week for the seeds to (4) _____. We learned that plants do not always grow from seeds. Some grow from (5) _____.

Life Science 14

Circle the term that fits the clue.

1. creating fuel from light:
   photosynthesis   chlorophyll

2. location of chlorophyll:
   root   leaf   trunk

3. gas created through photosynthesis:
   oxygen   hydrogen

4. green substance in leaves:
   carbon dioxide   chlorophyll

5. gas used in photosynthesis:
   carbon dioxide   oxygen

Life Science 15

Circle T for true or F for false.

1. Soil is a combination of crumbled rock, humus, air, and water. T F

2. Humus is a kind of dip eaten as a snack. T F

3. Compost can be used to enrich soils. T F

4. Peat usually forms in swamps or bogs. T F

Life Science Vocabulary

Life Science 16

Circle the term that best fits each clue.

1. related to breathing: digestion   respiration   excretion
2. related to breaking down food: digestion   respiration   excretion
3. waste disposal: digestion   respiration   excretion
4. transport of materials: digestion   circulation   regulation
5. many-celled: pituitary   temporal   multicellular

Life Science 17

Draw a line to match each term to the best clue.

1. beetle   not hatched from an egg
2. protoplasm   two species benefiting one another
3. mutualism   kind of insect
4. live birth   a species living at the expense of another
5. parasite   living matter

Life Science 18

Use the clues to unscramble the terms.

1. Animals that produce their own body heat are:

   arwm-bldeood _____.

2. Animals with segmented bodies and outer shells such as insects:

   rthroodsap _____

3. Bacteria that live in water and produce their own food through

   photosynthesis: **uebl-eegrn agael** _____

4. A creature's shell or hard protective layer: **esketonlxoe** _____

Life Science Vocabulary

Life Science 19

Write the word that best fits each clue.

**biome   physical   exchange
distribution   utility**

1. trade: _____

2. usefulness: _____

3. A grassland is an example of a

   _____.

4. A rock cracking is an example of

   a _____

   change.

5. spread: _____

Life Science 20

Draw a line to match each term to the best clue.

1. population   substances
2. source   group
3. convert   organization
4. structure   origin
5. materials   change

Life Science 21

Circle T for true or F for false.

1. Red blood cells are specialized to perform certain jobs. T F

2. Microorganisms live only on microscope lenses. T F

3. Pollination is often performed by 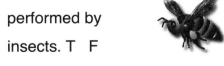 insects. T F

4. Gravity, wind, and animal activities help with seed dispersal. T F

Life Science 22

Write the word that best fits each clue.

**defend   descendant
survive   pest   protozoa**

1. single-celled organisms:

   _____

2. protect: _____

3. destructive animal or plant:

   _____

4. offspring: _____

5. continue to live:

   _____

Life Science Vocabulary

Life Science 23

Write the letter of the best word on each line.

A. nitrogen   B. osmosis   C. niche   D. nitrogen cycle

1. _____ is the movement of a fluid through a membrane.
2. A _____ is an organism's special place in an ecosystem.
3. Most of the gas in the atmosphere is _____.
4. As part of the _____, bacteria change a gas to a form plants can use.

Life Science 24

Circle the term that best fits the clue.
1. A clear, yellowish component of blood:
   sponge   crustacean   plasma
2. A marine animal: sponge   virus   spore
3. A single cell or seed that can grow into a new organism:
   spore   virus   plasma
4. An animal belonging to the same family as the lobster:
   sponge   crustacean   virus
5. A microscopic agent that can cause disease:
   crustacean   virus   plasma

Life Science 25

Draw a line to match each term to the best clue.

1. gills   outside

2. mates   inside

3. internal   reaction

4. external   goose and gander

5. response   respiratory organ of a fish

Human Body Vocabulary

Human Body 1

Write the term from the box that best fits each clue.

> abdomen
> forearm   instep
> thigh   calf

1. lower leg _____
2. lower arm _____
3. arched part of foot

   _____
4. upper leg _____
5. belly _____

Human Body 2

Fill in the missing letters.

1. a repeated series of events

   c __ c __ e
2. tissues grouped together to perform a function

   o __ __ __ n
3. a group of similar cells acting together to perform a function

   t __ s __ u __
4. organs grouped together to perform a function

   o __ g __ __   s __ __ t __ m

Human Body 3

Write the letter of the correct term on each line.

A. circulatory system
B. heart
C. cardiac
D. chambers
E. cardiac muscle

The word (1) _____ refers to a

special pump, the (2) _____. It is

an important part of the (3) _____.

It is made from (4) _____, and it has

four sections, or (5) _____.

Human Body 4

Circle the best term or terms for each clue.

1. carries used blood back to the heart:
   artery   capillary   vein
2. carries fresh blood from the heart to the body:
   artery   capillary   vein
3. carries oxygen and fuel to individual cells:
   artery   capillary   vein
4. blood vessel:
   artery   vein   platelets
5. carries blood from the heart to the lungs:
   capillary   pulmonary artery   vein

Human Body Vocabulary

Human Body 5

Fill in the missing letters.
1. Thickening of blood to stop bleeding:
   co __ g __ l __ t __ __ n
2. Blood cells that carry oxygen:
   r __ d
3. Blood cells that defend against outside invaders:
   w __ __ __ e
4. Cell fragments in plasma that help clotting:
   p __ __ te __ __ __ s
5. The clear liquid part of blood or lymph: p __ __ __ m __

Human Body 6

Write the letter of the correct term on each line.

A. spine   B. skeletal system
C. marrow   D. bones

The (1) _____ supports the body. It consists of the skull, (2) _____, and the (3) _____. Tissues inside the bones, in the (4) _____ produce blood cells. This system also includes joints and connective tissue.

Human Body 7

Circle the part of the body where each can be found.

1. femur: hips   arms   legs
2. pelvis: hips   arms   legs
3. patella: knee   elbow   heel
4. rib: chest   hips   skull
5. sternum: chest   knee   elbow

Human Body 8

Write the letter of the correct term on each line.

A. bronchial tubes   B. oxygen
C. lungs   D. respiratory system
E. diaphragm

The (1) _____ brings fresh (2) _____ into the body and carries away carbon dioxide. Powerful muscles in the (3) _____ expand the chest cavity to pull air into the (4) _____ through the (5) _____.

Human Body Vocabulary

Human Body 9

Using the clue, unscramble each boldface term.

1. brain and spinal cord:
   enalctr vusnero steysm _____
2. center for thought and control of body functions: **nrbai** _____
3. special cells that carry information: **snveer** _____
4. cord that carries information from the brain to body:
   alsinp rcod _____
5. something that causes a response: **ultimsus** _____

Human Body 10

Using the clue, unscramble each boldface term.

1. Breaks down food for use by cells in the body:
   evegtisdi _____ system
2. Pouch-like organ where food is broken down: **macohst** _____
3. Tube-like organ where food is digested and absorbed:
   nestestini _____
4. Tube from the mouth to the stomach: **ehagussop** _____
5. Releases substances that control the use of fuels from food:
   vrlie _____

Human Body 11

Using the clue, unscramble each boldface term.

1. Proteins, minerals, and vitamins are important
   utrintsen. _____
2. The food **miyrdpa** is a chart that helps people plan nutritious meals.
   _____
3. The body needs iron, calcium, and other **nalermis**. _____
4. A **eioalcr** is a measurement of food energy. _____
5. **Vnimita** C is important for good health. _____

Human Body Vocabulary

Human Body 12

Circle the correct term.

1. relating to the eye:

   optic   auditory   dental

2. relating to hearing:

   optic   auditory   dental

3. part of the tooth:

   retina   saliva   dentin

4. fluid in the mouth:

   retina   saliva   dentin

5. part of the eye:

   retina   saliva   dentin

Human Body 13

Fill in the missing letters.

1. This type of organ produces chemicals the body needs.

   g __ __ __ d

2. The glands of this system produce hormones.

   e __ __ oc __ __ n __

3. These glands release adrenaline.

   a __ __ e __ __ l

4. This gland produces insulin and digestive juices.

   p __ __ c __ __ __ s

Human Body 14

Draw a line to connect each clue to the correct term

1. system that moves waste out of the body

2. one of two organs that remove waste from blood

3. organ where urine is stored

4. organ that removes waste through perspiration

5. tube connecting bladder to the outside of the body

urethra

bladder

excretory

kidney

skin

Human Body 15

Circle T for true or F for false.

1. The biceps is found in the leg. T F

2. The triceps is found in the arm. T F

3. The muscular system breaks down food for the body. T F

4. When muscles relax, they get thicker and shorter. T F

5. When muscles contract, they get thicker and shorter. T F

Human Body Vocabulary

Human Body 16

Write the letter of the best term on each line.

**A. spleen   B. nodes   C. lymph
D. lymphatic system**

The job of the (1) _____ is to fight infection and maintain the body's fluid balance. It carries a fluid called (2) _____ from the tissues into the bloodstream. The (3) _____ produces cells that help to fight disease. Lymph (4) _____ help to filter bacteria and waste from the lymph fluid.

Human Body 17

Place the letter of the term on the blank next to the correct definition.

_____ 1. Breathing in
_____ 2. Breathing out
_____ 3. When the body takes in oxygen and releases carbon dioxide
_____ 4. Exhaled during respiration

**A. gas exchange
B. carbon dioxide
C. inhalation
D. exhalation**

Human Body 18

Circle T for true or F for false.

1. Starch is found in potatoes and rice. T F
2. All fiber is easy to digest. T   F
3. Proteins are macronutrients. T F
4. Vitamins are micronutrients. T F
5. Fats are unnecessary in a healthy diet. T   F

Human Body 19

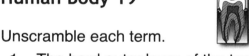

Unscramble each term.

1. The hard outer layer of the tooth
   eeamln _____
2. Tissue around the pulp inside the tooth
   etdinn _____
3. Part of the tooth below the gum
   orot _____
4. Part of the tooth above the gum line
   rnocw _____
5. Firm tissues around your teeth
   musg _____

Human Body Vocabulary

Human Body 20

Circle the term that fits each clue.

1.	Flat teeth designed for grinding	incisors	molars	deciduous
2.	Sharp teeth designed for cutting	incisors	molars	deciduous
3.	Teeth that fall out and are replaced	incisors	molars	deciduous
4.	Teeth that do not grow back if lost	dentures	deciduous	permanent
5.	Bones that hold the teeth	scapula	patella	jaw

Human Body 21

Unscramble each term.

1. Basic unit of heredity: **ngee** _____
2. Thread-like part of a cell that contains genes:
   roommosche _____
3. A molecule that contains coded hereditary information: **NDA** _____
4. Smallest particle of a particular compound or element:
   leulecmo _____
5. Traits passed from one generation to the next: **heyditer** _____

Human Body 22

Circle the best term to fit each clue.

1.	Light rays focus on rods and cones here.	lens	cornea	retina
2.	This flexible, clear structure controls focus in the eye.	lens	cornea	retina
3.	This is the colored part of the eye.	iris	lens	pupil
4.	This opening lets light into the eye.	iris	lens	pupil
5.	The clear outside coating of the eye.	cornea	iris	pupil

Human Body Vocabulary

Human Body 23

Fill in the missing letters.

1. one-celled organisms

   b ___ c ___ ___ r ___ a

2. vaccination to create immunity

   in ___ c ___ l ___ t ___ ___ n

3. a very tiny parasite or disease-causing agent v ___ ___ ___ s

4. a disease-causing agent

   p ___ ___ h ___ g ___ n

Human Body 24

Write the letter of the best term on each line.

A. infectious   **B. immune system**
C. lymphocytes **D. barriers**

The (1) _____ defends the body against (2) _____ diseases. Many (3) _____ guard the body, including the skin. (4) _____ in the bloodstream attack invaders.

Human Body 25

Unscramble each term.

1. good physical condition:

   esitfns _____

2. ease of movement:

   liibifltyxe _____

3. in the presence of oxygen:

   erabico _____

4. lasting power, stamina:

   edurennca _____

Human Body 26

Place the letter of the term next to the correct definition.

A. imaging   **B. prosthesis**
C. technology   **D. laser**
E. endoscope

____ 1. applied science

____ 2. making pictures of the inside of the body

____ 3. device for taking pictures inside the body

____ 4. device that replaces a body part

____ 5. produces a very powerful beam of light

Human Body Vocabulary

Human Body 27

Write the letter of the best term on each line.

A. sound waves   **B. vibrate**
C. eardrum   **D. impulses**
E. auditory canal

When (1) _____ enter the

(2) _____, they cause the

(3) _____ and tiny bones inside

the ear to (4) _____. Sensors in

the inner ear send (5) _____ to the

brain.

Human Body 28

Unscramble each term.

1. sense that lets you know where you are in space:
    bcealan _____

2. location of balance organs:
    nnier are _____

3. three tubular canals in the inner ear:
    laemsircuicr alsnac

    _____

4. part of the body that receives stimuli:
    nersos _____

Human Body 29

Circle the four basic tastes the taste buds can detect. Write a food for each taste.

1. spicy _____

2. sweet _____

3. sour _____

4. salty _____

5. bitter _____

Human Body 30

Draw a line matching each definition to its term.

1. causes a reaction   sensitive

2. hurt   irritation

3. receptive to feeling   pain

4. soreness or   dermis
    inflammation   stimulus

5. inner layer of skin

Earth Science Vocabulary

Earth Science 1

Write the best term for each clue.

outer core, mantle, crust, inner core

1. the outer layer of the earth

   _____

2. the center of the earth

   _____

3. just below the earth's outer layer

   _____

4. layer just above the earth's center

   _____

Earth Science 2

Unscramble each term.

1. recent theory that sections of the crust are in motion: plate
   icsetncto _____

2. a large land mass:
   ecoinntnt _____

3. older idea about the movement of the earth's continents:
   tlcnoeatnin rdtif

   _____

4. one of many large pieces of the earth's crust and upper mantle:
   apelt _____

Earth Science 3

Fill in the missing letters.

1. a crack in the rocky crust of the earth: f __ __ l __

2. shaking of the earth's surface caused by underground movement:

   e __ __ th __ __ a __ e

3. ripple of energy passing through rock, water, or air: w __ v __

4. machine that records ground movements:

   s __ __ s __ __ g __ __ __ h

Earth Science 4

Draw a line to match each term to the best clue.

1. seismology   size
2. shallow   shaking
3. tsunami   study of earthquakes
4. tremor   near the surface
5. magnitude   ocean wave caused by an earthquake

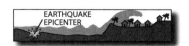

Earth Science Vocabulary

Earth Science 5

Fill in the missing letters.

1. relating to a volcano:

   v __ __ c __ __ ic

2. powdery rock from a volcanic

   explosion: a __ __

3. hard, dark rock formed from

   cooled lava: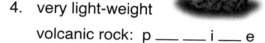

   b __ __ a __ t

4. very light-weight

   volcanic rock: p __ __ i __ e

5. glassy volcanic rock:

   ob __ __ d __ __ n

Earth Science 6

Write the letter for the correct term on each line.

A. crater B. chamber C. volcano D. magma   E. vent

A (1) _____ is a cone-shaped

mountain. It forms when (2) _____, or

molten rock, rises from a magma

(3) _____ to the surface. It flows out

through a (4) _____ at the top. After

the eruption, the top of the mountain

often caves in to form a (5) _____.

Earth Science 7

Circle the term that
matches each clue.

1. poisonous:

   toxic   explosive   volcanic

2. able to blow up:

   solidify   explosive   volcanic

3. turn into a solid:

   erupt   shield   solidify

4. outpouring of lava, ash, or gases:

   eruption   shield   composite

Earth Science 8

Match each term to the correct clue.

A. active B. dormant C. molten D. extinct   E. lava

____ 1. melted rock flowing on the
       surface

____ 2. adjective describing red-hot,
       liquid rock

____ 3. a volcano that will probably
       never erupt again

____ 4. a volcano that is not
       erupting at the moment

____ 5. a volcano that is erupting

Earth Science Vocabulary

Earth Science 9

Write the best word from the box on each line.

interior   exterior
epicenter   occur
seismometer

1. The part of the seismograph that measures the direction, duration, and force of an earthquake is a _____.
2. The inside of the earth is the _____.
3. The outside of the earth is the _____.
4. An earthquake's point of origin inside the earth is the _____.
5. Another word for "happen" is _____.

Earth Science 10

Write the best word from the box on each line.

igneous
metamorphic
pressure
sedimentary
rock cycle

The (1) _____ describes the way one kind of rock can change into another kind of rock. For example, layers of sandstone, a (2) _____ rock, can be melted deep inside the earth and flow out of a volcano to become basalt, an (3) _____ rock. That basalt can be buried under newer layers of rock. With heat and (4) _____, it can become a (5) _____, or changed, rock called a schist.

Earth Science 11

Fill in the missing letters.

1. Under heat and pressure, limestone changes to this metamorphic rock. m __ __ b __ e
2. Under heat and pressure, shale changes to this metamorphic rock.
   __ l __ t __
3. This igneous rock cools deep underground. g __ __ __ it __
4. rock form with a regular repeating structure: c __ __ __ t __ l
5. to change form: t __ __ __ __ f __ __ m

Earth Science Vocabulary

Earth Science 12

Write the correct term from the box on each blank.

fossilization	skeletons
impressions	hardened
shells	

During the process of (1) _____, plant and animal parts

are (2) _____ into rock. Fossilized (3) _____

of mammals, fish, birds, and reptiles tell us about life in the past.

(4) _____, such as dinosaur footprints, are fascinating fossils.

Fossilized (5) _____ of sea creatures are very common.

Earth Science 13

Unscramble each term.

1. Formations hanging from a cave ceiling:

   iteasttlacs _____

2. A formation on the floor of a cave: **saglitemta** _____

3. Another name for a cave: **vecran** _____

4. A substance capable of destroying or eating away:

   csiorerov _____

5. To mix with a liquid: **olsvdise** _____

Earth Science 14

Write the best word from the box on each line.

neap	tides	bulge
gravity	spring	

(1) _____ are caused by the (2) _____ of the moon

pulling on the earth's oceans. The water is pulled out into a (3) _____

on either side of the planet. When the sun and moon are lined up, there are

large tides called (4) _____ tides. When the sun and moon are

positioned at right angles, the tides are not as high as usual. These milder

changes in sea level are called (5) _____ tides.

Earth Science Vocabulary

Earth Science 15

Draw a line to match each sedimentary rock to its source.

1. sandstone   clay

2. conglomerate   sand

3. shale   dissolved shells

4. limestone   pebbles, sand, and clay

Earth Science 16

Write the best term on each line.
resistant, erosion, strata, conservation, weathering

1. layers of rock: _____
2. removal of rock by water or wind: _____
3. breaking up of rock by ice, rain, wind, or chemical action: _____
4. protecting soil from overuse or erosion: soil _____
5. able to stand up to erosion (a hard rock layer): _____

Earth Science 17

The following words are characteristics used to identify rocks and minerals. Unscramble each term.

1. lsture

   _____

2. sardhnes

   _____

3. olocr

   _____

4. satkre rlooc

   _____

5. tycrsla pehas

   _____

Earth Science 18

Fill in the missing letters.

1. The most common mineral on earth:

   q __ __ __ __ z
2. A natural substance with a crystalline structure:

   m __ n __ r __ l
3. A mineral used to make pennies:

   c __ p __ __ r
4. A mineral known as "fool's gold":

   p __ r __ t __
5. A yellow mineral that smells like rotten eggs: s __ lf __ r

Earth Science Vocabulary

Earth Science 19

Draw a line to match each term with an example.

1. renewable resource
2. nonrenewable resource
3. alternative energy source
4. pollution

wind energy

smog

forests

oil

Earth Science 20

Fill in the missing letters.

1. Hard coal that burns at a high temperature:

   a __ t __ r __ c __ __ e

2. Soft coal that burns at lower temperatures:

   b __ t __ __ i __ o __ s

3. Parts of living things turned to rock, coal, or petroleum:

   fo __ __ i __ s

Earth Science 21

Write the letter of the correct word on the line.

A. topography, B. lithosphere, C. block, D. folded

_____ 1. Mountains that are pushed up between two faults

_____ 2. Mountains built from bent rock layers

_____ 3. The top rocky layer of the crust

_____ 4. The surface features of an area

Earth Science 22

Circle the correct term.

1. pushed up:

   compressed   deposited   uplifted

2. in the open:

   exposed   compressed   deposited

3. laid down:

   uplifted   deposited   compressed

4. pushed together:

   uplifted   deposited   compressed

Earth Science Vocabulary

Earth Science 23

Write the letter of the correct term on the line.

A. dunes   **B. crescent**
C. particles   **D. deposited**

1. Sand _____ come in several shapes.
2. Sand is composed of rock _____.
3. Many dunes are _____- shaped.
4. The sand is carried and _____ by the wind.

Earth Science 24

Unscramble each term.

1. large floating chunk of ice:

   ibeegrc _____
2. melting glacier:

   rtreangeti _____
3. growing glacier:

   acianndvg _____
4. U-shaped area created by a glacier: **lyeval** _____
5. type of glacier that covers large areas of Antarctica:

   cie hsete _____

Earth Science 25

Fill in the missing letters.

1. near the ocean:

   c __ a __ t __ l
2. curved rock formation formed by erosion: a __ __ h
3. rock column in the ocean near the shore: s __ __ __ k
4. waves wearing away the lower part of a cliff:

   u __ __ er __ __ t __ __ ng

Earth Science 26

Write the letter for the best term on each line.

**A. ground water, B. columns,
C. surface streams, D. formations,
E. chambers**

Limestone caverns are often filled with beautiful (1) _____. Natural (2) _____ dissolves the rock to create underground rooms called (3) _____. Stalactites, stalagmites, and (4) _____ are like magical gardens of stone. Sometimes (5) _____ plunge down through openings to form waterfalls.

Earth Science Vocabulary

Earth Science 27

Write the letter of the best word on each line.

**A. abyssal   B. slope   C. shelf
D. seaward   E. floor**

The ocean (1) _____ is deeper in some places than others. The continental (2) _____ lies underwater at the edge of each continent. Beyond it, in deeper water, is the continental (3) _____. On the (4) _____ side of the slope is the (5) _____ plain.

Earth Science 28

Fill in the missing letters.

1. A consistent flow of surface water is an ocean

   c ___ ___ ___ e ___ t.

2. The d ___ ___ t ___ of the ocean varies from shallow shelves to deep trenches.

3. The saltiness of the ocean is called its s ___ l ___ ___ ___ t ___.

4. The word m ___ r ___ ___ e refers to the ocean.

Earth Science 29

Draw a line to match each clue to the correct term.

1. the deepest parts of the ocean floor   hot spot

2. not deep   island

3. top   trenches

4. land surrounded by water   shallow

5. place where volcanic islands form   surface

Earth Science 30

Circle the correct term.

1. middle of the ocean:

   sonar   mid-ocean

2. area:

   zone   sonar

3. used to find underwater objects:

   sonar   catapult

4. ocean bottom:

   zone   sea floor

5. landmass:

   sea floor   continent

Earth Science Vocabulary

Earth Science 31

Unscramble each term

1. A deep crack in a glacier:

   sevacres _____

2. To crush:

   mptcaco _____

3. Loose rock fragments:

   ebrisd _____

4. Large loose rocks:

   oulbders _____

Earth Science 32

Circle T for true or F for false.

1. Floodplains are found on steep mountainsides.
   T F

2. A delta forms where a large river enters the ocean. T F

3. A river meander is an area with many rapids. T F

4. A canyon is a narrow valley with steep walls. T F

5. A river system includes the source, the tributaries, and the mouth. T F

Earth Science 33

Draw a line to match each clue to the best term.

1. any precious stone
2. the hardest stone
3. fossilized tree sap
4. a purple stone
5. a green gem

   amethyst
   emerald
   gem
   amber
   diamond

Earth Science 34

Circle the term that best fits each clue.

1. large dark green seaweed:

   kelp   plankton   diatom

2. under the ocean:

   coastal   undersea   hydrothermal

3. constructive:

   unchanging   breaking down   building up

4. destructive:

   unchanging   breaking down   building up

Atmospheric & Space Science Vocabulary

Atmospheric & Space Science 1

Circle T for true or F for false.

1. Air pressure is the weight of air pushing down. T F
2. Falling rain is an example of evaporation. T F
3. The earth's atmosphere is composed of gases. T F
4. The weather is the current condition of outdoor air. T F
5. A rainstorm is an example of climate. T F

Atmospheric & Space Science 2

Draw a line to match each instrument to what it measures.

1. anemometer   air pressure
2. barometer   temperature
3. hygrometer   precipitation
4. thermometer   humidity
5. rain gauge   wind speed

Atmospheric & Space Science 3

Unscramble each term.

1. A small rocky body orbiting the sun: **teroidas** _____
2. An icy body with a long tail orbiting the sun:

   otcme _____
3. Rock or metal from space entering the earth's atmosphere:

   eormet _____
4. Part of a meteor that lands on earth:

   etemoriet _____

Atmospheric & Space Science 4

Fill in the missing letters.

1. A group of bright stars associated with a story:

   c __ __ st __ __ la __ i __ n
2. A large group of stars:

   g __ l __ __ y
3. A large sphere of burning gas in space:

   s __ __ __
4. A collapsed star with extremely powerful gravity:

   b __ __ __ k h __ __ e

Atmospheric & Space Science Vocabulary

Atmospheric & Space Science 5

Circle the term that matches each clue.

1.	long dry period:	pollution	ozone	drought
2.	greenhouse effect:	global warming	global cooling	pollution
3.	a form of oxygen:	nitrogen	drought	ozone
4.	man-made impurities:	pollution	nitrogen	drought
5.	world-wide:	local	coastal	global

Atmospheric & Space Science 6

Circle the best term for each definition.

1. a scientist who studies the universe: cosmologist   geologist
2. to fall in: retreat   collapse
3. planets orbiting a star: solar system   local group
4. the universe: Milky Way   everything in space
5. the most common element in the universe: oxygen   hydrogen
6. a light gas that does not burn: helium   nickel

Atmospheric & Space Science 7

Unscramble each boldface term.

1. Cooler dark spots on the surface of the sun are called **otnssups**. _____
2. A powerful explosion in the sun's atmosphere is a solar **elfar**. _____
3. During a total solar eclipse, the sun's **roacno** _____ is visible.
4. When the moon comes between the sun and the earth, there is a solar **lipeesc**. _____
5. The invisible light waves responsible for sunburns are called **oleurtavilt** _____ rays.

Atmospheric & Space Science Vocabulary

Atmospheric & Space Science 8

Circle the term that best fits each clue.

1. Mars, Venus, Earth:

    outer planets   inner planets

2. revolve around another body:

    orbit   collapse

3. Neptune, Saturn, Jupiter:

    outer planets   inner planets

4. a large body circling a star:

    comet   planet

Atmospheric & Space Science 9

Fill in the missing letters.

The four (1) __ n __ er

p __ __ n __ __ s are also called

the (2) r __ __ __ y, or terrestrial,

planets. They are

(3) M __ __ c __ r __,

(4) V __ __ __ __,

(5) E __ __ __ __ , and

(6) M __ __ __.

Atmospheric & Space Science 10

Fill in the missing letters.

The four (1) __ u __ e __ planets

are also called the

(2) g __ s __ o __ s planets.

They are (3) J __ p __ t __ r,

(4) S __ t __ r __,

(5) U __ __ n __ s,

and (6) N __ __ t __ __ e.

Atmospheric & Space Science 11

Draw a line to match each clue to the best term.

1. our galaxy   telescope

2. instrument to see

    distant objects   local group

3. grouped close

    together   nebula

4. galaxies close to

    the Milky Way   Milky Way

5. a cloud of stars,

    gas, and dust

    in space   cluster

Atmospheric & Space Science Vocabulary

Atmospheric & Space Science 12

Fill in the missing letters.

1. The earth spins around its ax __ __.

2. G __ __ __ ity pulls things toward the earth's surface.

3. The r __ t __ t __ __ n of the earth causes day and night.

4. The earth's r __ __ __ l __ t __ __ n around the sun takes a year.

Atmospheric & Space Science 13

Write the letter of the best word on each line.

A. Hemisphere   **B. equator**
C. seasons   **D. tilt**

The (1) _____ of the earth's axis causes the (2) _____. When it is winter in the Northern (3) _____, it is summer in the Southern Hemisphere. The (4) _____ separates the Northern Hemisphere from the Southern Hemisphere.

Atmospheric & Space Science 14

Fill in the missing letters.

The Milky Way is a

(1) b __ __ re __

(2) s __ __ r __ l galaxy.

Many other galaxies are

(3) e __ __ __ pti __ __ __.

Sometimes, galaxies

(4) c __ __ l __ d __, or run into each other.

Atmospheric & Space Science 15

Circle the term that best fits each clue.

1. a rotating neutron star:
   supernova   pulsar

2. a stage in the death of a medium-sized star:
   red giant   neutron star

3. the sudden brief explosion of a star:
   pulsar   supernova

4. a bright object at the edge of the universe:
   red giant   quasar

Atmospheric & Space Science Vocabulary

Atmospheric & Space Science 16

Place the letter of the term next to the correct definition.

A. astronomer   **B. imaginary**
C. Orion   **D. constellation**
E. Ursa Major

____ 1. group of stars connected with a story

____ 2. scientist who studies stars

____ 3. mythic

____ 4. constellation, the great bear

____ 5. constellation, the hunter

Atmospheric & Space Science 17

Fill in the missing letters.

1. very small planets, including Pluto: d __ a __ f planets

2. an area at the edge of the solar system:
   K __ __ p __ r b __ __ t

3. an area of space between Mars and Jupiter: a __ __ e __ __ id b __ __ t

4. a crater caused by a meteorite: __ __ __ a __ t crater

5. objects in space:
   b __ __ __ __ s

Atmospheric & Space Science 18

Circle T for true or F for false.

1. A droplet is a very large water drop. T F

2. Fog consists of water droplets suspended in the air. T F

3. Smog is fog mixed with smoke or other pollutants. T F

4. A drizzle is a heavy downpour. T F

5. If the air is moist, it is extremely dry. T F

Atmospheric & Space Science 19

Unscramble the terms.

1. light waves invisible to humans; used in remote controls:
   nfridare _____

2. different forms of the same thing:
   rinsativao _____

3. an element present in living things:
   arbnco _____

4. to move around:
   ctelircua _____

Atmospheric & Space Science Vocabulary

Atmospheric & Space Science 20

Write the correct term from the box
on each line.

warm front	transpiration
cold front	El Niño
evaporation	

1. a warm ocean current that creates unusual weather _____

2. a cool air mass moving in on a warm air mass _____

3. a warm air mass moving in on a cool air mass _____

4. water vapor moving into the air through the leaves of plants

   _____

5. to change from a liquid to a gas _____

Atmospheric & Space Science 21

Circle the best term for each description.

1. large tropical storm with high winds and heavy rain:
   hurricane   tornado   front

2. a powerful funnel-shaped wind storm:
   hurricane   tornado   front

3. rainstorm with thunder and lightning:
   hurricane   thunderstorm   front

4. discharge of electricity from clouds:
   front   magnetism   lightning

5. where two different air masses meet:
   front   tornado   hurricane

6. a body of warm or cool air:
   hurricane   tornado   air mass

Atmospheric & Space Science Vocabulary

Atmospheric & Space Science 22

Circle the correct term to match the definition.

1. High clouds, often made of ice:
   cumulus   stratus   cirrus
2. Low, fluffy-looking clouds:
   cumulus   stratus   cirrus
3. An even blanket of low gray clouds:
   cumulus   stratus   cirrus
4. Mid-level clouds in bunches:
   altocumulus   cirrus   nimbus
5. Rainclouds:
   altocumulus   cirrus   nimbus

Atmospheric & Space Science 23

Unscramble each term.

1. Rain, hail, and snow:
   pipitaorectin _____
2. Repeating periods of heat and cold:
   weather **tprnate** _____
3. ice chunks:
   ihla _____
4. ice crystals:
   nsow _____
5. liquid water drops:
   arin _____

Atmospheric & Space Science 24

Circle T for true or F for false.

1. Humidity is a kind of mud caused by heavy runoff. T F
2. In determining relative humidity, temperature is important. T F
3. The dew point is a temperature. T F
4. Precipitation is part of the water cycle. T F

Atmospheric & Space Science 25

Place the letter of the correct word in each blank.

A. lunar   B. eclipse   C. moon
D. phases   E. quarter

The (1) _____ rotates around the earth. The word (2) _____ is an adjective that means "relating to the moon." The moon's shapes, or (3) _____, include full, half, and (4) _____. Sometimes, the shadow of the earth causes a strange phenomenon called an (5) _____.

Physical Science Vocabulary

Physical Science 1

Circle the best term for each clue.

1. practical knowledge:

   fiber   technology   consumption

2. thread:

   metal   gas   fiber

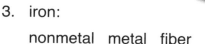

3. iron:

   nonmetal   metal   fiber

4. carbon:

   nonmetal   metal   gas

5. precious metal:

   iron   tin   gold

Physical Science 2

Unscramble each term.

1. blocks all light (wood):

   uepoqa _____

2. can be seen through (glass):

   antrarenspt

   _____

3. light passes through (tracing paper):

   tnanslrceut

   _____

4. separates white light into a spectrum:

   ipmrs _____

Physical Science 3

Circle the best term for each clue.

1. a lens curved inward:

   concave   convex   hollow

2. a lens curved outward:

   concave   convex   hollow

3. ability to soak up:

   refraction   reflection   absorption

4. wave changes direction:

   refraction   reflection   absorption

5. wave bounces from a surface:

   refraction   reflection   absorption

Physical Science 4

Draw a line to match each clue to the correct term.

1. enlarge   telescope

2. instrument to see   lens
   faraway things   binoculars

3. instrument to see   microscope
   very small things   magnify

4. instrument with
   two enlarging
   lenses

5. glass curved to
   bend light

Physical Science Vocabulary

Physical Science 5

Fill in the missing letters.

1. to swing back and forth rhythmically:

   o ___ ci ___ ___ a ___ ___

2. extreme point on a pendulum swing:

   a ___ ___ li ___ u ___ e

3. repeating:

   r ___ ___ e ___ ___ t ___ on

4. number of times something happens in a given amount of time:

   f ___ ___ ___ u ___ ___ c ___

Physical Science 6

Circle the best term for each example.

1. iron: metal   alloy   nonmetal

2. molten: metal   melted   feathery

3. quartz: metal   alloy   nonmetal

4. studies metals:

   geologist   metallurgist

5. brass: nonmetal   alloy   copper

Physical Science 7

Circle the numbers of the statements that are true.

1. H_2O is the chemical formula for water.

2. Flammability is an example of a chemical property.

3. An ice cube melting is a chemical change.

4. Water evaporating is a physical change.

5. Length is an example of a physical property.

Physical Science 8

Circle the best term to fit each example.

1. vinegar:

   acid   base   litmus

2. baking soda:

   acid   base   litmus

3. ammonia:

   acid   base   litmus

4. test paper:

   acid   base   litmus

5. lemon juice:

   acid   base   litmus

Physical Science Vocabulary

Physical Science 9

Fill in the missing letters.

1. colors in white light: sp __ __ t __ __ m
2. wavelengths between light and radio waves: i __ __ __ ar __ d
3. invisible waves that cause sunburns: ul __ __ a __ __ ol __ t
4. colorful arc in sky created by refraction: r __ __ n __ __ w
5. the study of light: o __ __ i __ s

Physical Science 10

Circle T for true or F for false.

1. The speed of sound is faster than the speed of light. T F
2. Vibration is fast side-to-side movement. T F
3. The loudness or softness of a musical note is its pitch. T F
4. A sonic boom happens when an airplane goes faster than the speed of sound. T F
5. When you travel at a subsonic speed, you are underwater. T F
6. When you travel at a supersonic speed, you are in a slow car. T F

Physical Science 11

Fill in each blank with a term from the box.

element   atom   properties
molecule   Periodic Table

1. An _____ has a nucleus and electrons.
2. A water _____ has two hydrogen atoms and one oxygen atom.
3. Hydrogen is an _____. All of its atoms are hydrogen atoms.
4. The _____ is a chart showing all of the elements.
5. Water has important physical and chemical _____.

Physical Science Vocabulary

Physical Science 12

Fill in the missing letters.

1. A c ___ ___ p ___ n ___ ___ t is part of something.
2. A c ___ mp ___ ___ n ___ is a chemical combination of elements.
3. In a m ___ ___ t ___ ___ e, substances combine without a chemical reaction.
4. Salt dissolved in water is a s ___ l ___ t ___ ___ n.
5. Muddy water is a su ___ p ___ ns ___ ___ n.

Physical Science 13

Circle the best term for each description.

1. oxygen in the air:
   liquid   solid   gas
2. water at room temperature:
   liquid   solid   gas
3. ice: liquid   solid   gas
4. to change from solid to liquid:
   solidify   evaporate   melt
5. to change from liquid to solid:
   solidify   evaporate   melt

Physical Science 14

Use the clues to unscramble each term.

1. draw toward:
   tatactr _____
2. push away:
   perel _____
3. indicates magnetic north:
   mpacsos _____
4. plus:
   opvesiti _____
5. minus:
   egiveatn _____

Physical Science 15

Match the letter of each term to its definition.

A. neutron, B. proton, C. particle, D. nucleus, E. matter

____ 1. a positively charged particle

____ 2. a particle, neither positively nor negatively charged

____ 3. the center of an atom

____ 4. unit of matter (atom, molecule, proton)

____ 5. substance

Physical Science Vocabulary

Physical Science 16

Write the letter for the best word on each line.

A. current   **B. conductor**
C. amp   **D. battery**

1. An _____ is a basic unit of electricity.
2. A _____ changes chemical energy into electrical energy.
3. Copper is a good _____ of electricity.
4. Electrical _____ flows through the wires.

Physical Science 17

Unscramble each term.

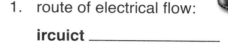

1. route of electrical flow:
   ircuict _____
2. safety device to cut the flow of electricity:
   circuit **abrreke** _____
3. device that reduces or prevents flow of electricity:
   utlainsor _____

Physical Science 18

Fill in the missing letters.

1. speed up:
   a __ __ el __ r __ te
2. slow down:
   d __ c __ l __ r __ t __
3. speed in a certain direction:
   v __ l __ c __ t __
4. forward motion and resistance to slowing:
   m __ __ e __ t __ m

Physical Science 19

Unscramble each term

1. energy of a moving object:
   etinikc _____
2. unmoving: **ranaoytist**
   _____
3. changing energy from one form to another: **onvcoersin**
   _____
4. energy of an object at rest:
   tienptaol _____

Physical Science Vocabulary

Physical Science 20

Write the best term from the box on each line.

coal	nonrenewable
energy	fossil fuels
petroleum	

We use (1) _____ to power our cars and

generate electricity. Most of the fuels we use today were

created deep inside the earth. They are called

(2) _____. Layers of

(3) _____ formed from buried peat bogs. Pools

of (4) _____ formed from the remains of tiny prehistoric sea

creatures. Once oil has been used, it cannot be replaced, so it is a

(5) _____ resource.

Physical Science 21

Read each term. Circle the best example.

1. simple machine	car	locomotive	wheel and axle
2. wedge	hook	ax	teeter-totter
3. lever	hook	ax	teeter-totter
4. inclined plane	ramp	wheel and axle	pulley
5. complex machine	ramp	scissors	wheel and axle

Physical Science Vocabulary

Physical Science 22

Fill in the missing letters.

1. Extra heat given off by machines as they work is w __ __ __ e heat.

2. Energy cannot be created or d __ __ tr __ y __ d.

3. H __ __ t is a form of energy.

4. H __ dr __ __ l __ __ tri __ i __ ty is water power.

Physical Science 23

Circle the best definition for each term.

1. work:

   sweat   transfer energy

2. generate:

   create   use

3. renewable:

   irreplaceable   replaceable

4. additional:

   supplemental   mathematical

Physical Science 24

Fill in the missing letters to list alternative energy sources.

1. g __ __ th __ __ __ al

2. n __ __ l __ __ __ r

3. w __ __ __

4. so __ __ __

5. hy __ __ __ el __ __ tr __ c

Physical Science 25

Match the letter of the term to the correct definition.

A. friction, B. inertia, C. energy, D. force, E. motion

___ 1. ability to do work

___ 2. stops or moves an object

___ 3. resistance between two moving objects

___ 4. movement

___ 5. resisting change

Science & Technology Vocabulary

Science & Technology 1

Circle the best word to match each clue.

1. air resistance: lift   airfoil   drag
2. pressure of air pushing a wing up: weight   lift   thrust
3. curved shape of the top of a wing: thrust   drag   airfoil
4. force experienced because of gravity: weight   thrust   lift
5. forward push: lift   thrust   airfoil

Science & Technology 2

Unscramble each term associated with nuclear reactions.

1. breaking apart the nucleus of an atom to release energy:
   snsiofi _____
2. giving off energetic particles:
   rdioctaivea _____
3. element used in some nuclear power plants:
   aumnuri _____
4. particle that strikes and breaks apart a nucleus in a chain reaction:
   tonuenr _____

Science & Technology 3

Fill in the missing letters.

1. A network for distributing power is a g __ __ d.
2. The electricity delivered to your house is a __ t __ __ n __ t __ __ g current.
3. Cables are part of the power d __ __ tr __ b __ t __ __ n system.
4. Before arriving at our home, electricity passed through a local s __ __ s __ __ t __ __ n.

Science & Technology 4

Write the letter of the correct word on each line.

**A. telegraph   B. transmit   C. Morse
D. Marconi   E. device**

Samuel (1) _____ developed a code for the (2) _____, an electrical (3) _____ designed to (4) _____ messages over a wire. Guglielmo (5) _____ is famous for his work on the radio, a way to send information through the air without a wire.

Science & Technology Vocabulary

Science & Technology 5

Circle T for true or F for false.

1. Telecommunication is another word for a television news report. T F
2. An amplifier makes a signal more powerful. T F
3. An antenna can be used to send or receive radio signals. T F
4. A communications satellite is always located on top of a hill. T F
5. If a station transmits television signals, it is broadcasting. T F

Science & Technology 6

Fill in the missing letters.

1. Thomas Edison created the first practical
   ph __ __ __ g __ __ __ hic recordings.
2. A m __ g __ __ t __ c recording is stored on a special tape.
3. A d __ g __ t __ l recording is read by a laser.
4. The letters in the word
   l __ __ __ r stand for light amplification by stimulated emission of radiation.

Science & Technology 7

Unscramble each term.

1. A clock with a face and hands is an **laoang**
   _____ device.
2. A clock with numbers that change is a **giiatdl**
   _____ device.
3. A **itb** _____ can be either 0 or 1.
4. A **teyb** _____ is eight **sitb** _____.

Science & Technology 8

Fill in the missing letters to match each clue.

1. controls the flow of electricity in electronic devices:
   tra __ __ i __ t __ r
2. common element used in making semiconductors:
   s __ l __ c __ n
3. special chip that performs basic computer operations:
   m __ c __ opr __ c __ ss __ r
4. tiny silicon wafer with an integrated circuit: c __ __ p

Science & Technology Vocabulary

Science & Technology 9

Circle T for true or F for false.

1. Printers, scanners, and cameras are peripherals. T F
2. A monitor is a kind of keyboard. T F
3. A page being printed from the computer is input. T F
4. A letter being typed into a word processing program is output. T F

Science & Technology 10

Unscramble each term.

1. data:

   iatioronfmn _____

2. a structured collection of information:

   taasabde _____

3. a system of linked computers:

   nerktwo _____

4. directions telling a computer how to perform a task:

   rparogm _____

Science & Technology 11

Fill in the missing letters.

1. the first workable model of a manufactured item:

   p __ __ t __ t __ __ e

2. eye scans and fingerprint keys are examples of:

   b __ __ m __ tr __ __ s

3. making machines very small:

   m __ niat __ ri __ at __ __ n

Science & Technology 12

Circle the best term.

1. material composed of plant cell walls:

   synthetic   cellulose

2. to reuse: recycle   synthesize

3. crushed wood used in papermaking: polyester   pulp

4. a moving belt that transports materials: conveyor   turbine

Science & Technology Vocabulary

Science & Technology 13

Write the letter of the correct scientist on each line.

**A. Pasteur B. Curie
C. Pascal D. Franklin E. Faraday**

_____ 1. founder of electrochemistry

_____ 2. demonstrated that microbes cause disease

_____ 3. discovered radioactivity

_____ 4. proposed that electricity flowed

_____ 5. studied fluid pressure and invented the barometer

Science & Technology 14

Unscramble each term.

1. Field biologists track wolves with radio **smrtarsteitn**. _____

2. The **lznidseatniaio** _____ process creates fresh water from salt water.

3. **tnevsanocori** _____ practices help preserve natural resources.

4. Something added to the environment that is harmful to living things is called **oplinoutl**. _____

Science & Technology 15

Circle T for true or F for false.

1. Compost is decayed plant matter. T F

2. Generating energy from ocean waves is called incineration. T F

3. Methane is an endangered rain forest plant. T F

4. A landfill is a waste-management facility. T F

5. Junk yards recover scrap metals. T F

Science & Technology 16

Fill in the missing letters.

1. Using DNA information to change plants and animals is g __ n __ t __ c engineering.

2. P __ st __ c __ d __ s kill insects that destroy crops, but they can harm wildlife.

3. B __ __ l __ g __ c __ l pest control is a way to protect crops without insecticides.

Science & Technology Vocabulary

Science & Technology 17

Write the best word or phrase from the box on each line.

windmills	harness
reserves	turbine
wind farm	

1. Spinning rotor blades in a _____ change steam to electricity.
2. Oil _____ will not last forever.
3. Scientists are working to _____ the power of the wind.
4. On the great plains, farmers used _____ to pump water from wells.
5. A _____ near us uses several windmills to contribute clean energy to the grid.

Rotor Blades

Science & Technology 18

Circle the best term to fit each clue.

1. information sent: signal   modem   decode
2. changes computer data to phone signals: vacuum tubes   modem   circuit
3. a set of symbols used to talk to a computer: chip   conductor   code
4. using integrated circuits or transistors: insulated   electronic   portable
5. to change information into usable form: decode   signal   fetch

Science & Technology 19

Circle the scientist who fits each famous discovery.

1. Proposed that the earth rotated around the sun: Mendel   Copernicus   Einstein
2. Improved the refracting telescope: Newton   Mendel   Galileo
3. Developed three laws of motion: Newton   Mendel   Galileo
4. Discovered principles of heredity: Newton   Mendel   Einstein
5. Formulated the General Theory of Relativity: Newton   Mendel   Einstein

Answer Keys

General Science 1 (p. 2)
1. particle   2. method
3. science   4. expand
5. contract

General Science 2 (p. 2)
1. fact   2. system
3. cause   4. effect

General Science 3 (p. 2)
1. concept, idea
2. observe, watch
3. compare, find similarities
4. contrast, find differences
5. record, write down or save

General Science 4 (p. 2)
1. conclusion   2. data
3. collect   4. analysis   5. logic

General Science 5 (p. 3)
1. theory   2. hypothesis
3. experiment   4. identify
5. repeat

General Science 6 (p. 3)
1. word   2. mesh
3. basic   4. complicated
5. combination

General Science 7 (p. 3)
1. investigate   2. technique
3. measure   4. condition
5. substance

General Science 8 (p. 4)
1. state, temporary form
2. force, energy
3. fundamental, basic
4. flow, move
5. unit, part

General Science 9 (p. 4)
1. Finite   2. Infinite
3. Supplemental
4. phenomenon

General Science 10 (p. 4)
1. F 2. T 3. F 4. T 5. F

General Science 11 (p. 4)
1. instrument   2. happen
3. plentiful   4. beginning
5. change

General Science 12 (p. 5)
1. density   2. speed
3. mass   4. volume
5. weight

General Science 13 (p. 5)
1. True   2. False   3. True   4. False

General Science 14 (p. 5)
1. kilogram, a thousand grams
2. gram, basic metric unit of weight
3. milligram, a thousandth of a gram
4. millimeter, a thousandth of a meter
5. centimeter, a hundredth of a meter

General Science 15 (p. 6)
1. temperature   2. Celsius
3. degree   4. Fahrenheit

General Science 16 (p. 6)
1. absorb   2. balance
3. buoyancy   4. characteristic
5. classify

General Science 17 (p. 6)
1. width, diameter
2. most important, dominant
3. judge results, evaluate
4. data supporting a conclusion, evidence
5. diagram showing steps, flow chart

General Science 18 (p. 6)
1. function   2. inference
3. investigate   4. metric
5. model

General Science 19 (p. 7)
1. movement   2. thing
3. noticing   4. stage
5. foretell

General Science 20 (p. 7)
1. constant   2. variable
3. decay   4. average

General Science 21 (p. 7)
1. equilibrium 2. imbalance

General Science 22 (p. 7)
1. reasonable 2. quantify
3. increase 4. response

General Science 23 (p. 8)
1. purpose 2. sequence
3. property
4. scientific explanations
5. scientific procedures

General Science 24 (p. 8)
1. Venn diagram 2. volume
3. thriving 4. variables
5. transfer

General Science 25 (p. 9)
1. stable 2. structure
3. technique 4. system

General Science 26 (p. 9)
1. sequence 2. result
3. precise 4. segment
5. name

General Science 27 (p. 9)
1. T 2. F 3. T 4. F 5. F

General Science 28 (p. 9)
1. study 2. series
3. test 4. valid

General Science 29 (p. 10)
1. scientific law
2. scientific model
3. scientific theory
4. scientific method
5. scientific evidence

General Science 30 (p. 10)
1. regulate 2. random
3. reject 4. dehydrate
5. cyclic

General Science 31 (p. 11)
1. collide, run into each other
2. absolute, does not change
3. principles, fundamental rules or laws
4. relative, depends upon changing conditions

General Science 32 (p. 11)
1. T 2. F 3. F 4. T

General Science 33 (p. 11)
1. frequency
2. interrelationship
3. probable
4. recede
5. advance

General Science 34 (p. 11)
1. replicate, copy
2. submerge, sink
3. boundary, limit
4. inorganic, nonliving
5. significance, importance

Life Science 1 (p. 12)
1. classification 2. nonliving
3. organisms 4. species

Life Science 2 (p. 12)
1. carnivores 2. herbivores
3. omnivores

Life Science 3 (p. 12)
1. T 2. F 3. T 4. T 5. F

Life Science 4 (p. 12)
1. mammal, has fur or hair
2. reptile, has scales
3. amphibian, lives part of life on land and part in water
4. bird, has feathers
5. mollusk, is an invertebrate

Life Science 5 (p. 13)
1. ecology 2. community
3. biosphere 4. environment
5. adaptation

Life Science 6 (p. 13)
1. camouflage 2. prey
3. mimicry 4. extinction
5. predator

Life Science 7 (p. 13)
1. ovary 2. stigma
3. pollen 4. petal 5. pistil

Life Science 8 (p. 14)
1. calf 2. eye color
3. diving 4. forest 5. kitten

Life Science 9 (p. 14)
1. C 2. A 3. D 4. B

Life Science 10 (p. 14)
1. membrane, a thin wall or layer
2. cytoplasm, contents of a cell, except the nucleus
3. cell, a basic unit of life
4. organelles, tiny structures with special tasks
5. nucleus, control center of a cell

Life Science 11 (p. 14)
1. F 2. T 3. T 4. F 5. F

Life Science 12 (p. 15)
1. branch, crown   3. cone
4. needle, limb

Life Science 13 (p. 15)
1. D 2. A 3. C 4. B 5. E

Life Science 14 (p. 15)
1. photosynthesis 2. leaf
3. oxygen   4. chlorophyll
5. carbon dioxide

Life Science 15 (p. 15)
1. T 2. F 3. T 4. T

Life Science 16 (p. 16)
1. respiration   2. digestion
3. excretion   4. circulation
5. multicellular

Life Science 17 (p. 16)
1. beetle, kind of insect
2. protoplasm, living matter
3. mutualism, two species benefiting one another
4. live birth, not hatched from an egg
5. parasite, a species living at the expense of another

Life Science 18 (p. 16)
1. warm-blooded   2. arthropods
3. blue-green algae 4. exoskeleton

Life Science 19 (p. 17)
1. exchange   2. utility
3. biome   4. physical
5. distribution

Life Science 20 (p. 17)
1. population, group
2. source, origin
3. convert, change
4. structure, organization
5. materials, substances

Life Science 21 (p. 17)
1. T 2. F 3. T 4. T

Life Science 22 (p. 17)
1. protozoa   2. defend   3. pest
4. descendant 5. survive

Life Science 23 (p. 18)
1. B 2. C 3. A 4. D

Life Science 24 (p. 18)
1. plasma   2. sponge
3. spore   4. crustacean
5. virus

Life Science 25 (p. 18)
1. gills, respiratory organ of a fish
2. mates, goose and gander
3. internal, inside
4. external, outside
5. response, reaction

Human Body 1 (p. 19)
1. calf   2. forearm
3. instep 4. thigh
5. abdomen

Human Body 2 (p. 19)
1. cycle   2. organ
3. tissue 4. organ system

Human Body 3 (p. 19)
1. C 2. B 3. A 4. E 5. D

Human Body 4 (p. 19)
1. vein   2. artery
3. capillary 4. artery, vein
5. pulmonary artery

Human Body 5 (p. 20)
1. coagulation 2. red
3. white   4. platelets
5. plasma

Human Body 6 (p. 20)
1. B 2. D/A 3. A/D 4. C

Human Body 7 (p. 20)
1. legs   2. hips   3. knee
4. chest   5. chest

Human Body 8 (p. 20)
1. D 2. B 3. E 4. C 5. A

Human Body 9 (p. 21)
1. central nervous system
2. brain   3. nerves
4. spinal cord   5. stimulus

Human Body 10 (p. 21)
1. digestive   2. stomach
3. intestines   4. esophagus
5. liver

Human Body 11 (p. 21)
1. nutrients   2. pyramid
3. minerals   4. calorie
5. Vitamin

Human Body 12 (p. 22)
1. optic   2. auditory
3. dentin   4. saliva   5. retina

Human Body 13 (p. 22)
1. gland   2. endocrine
3. adrenal   4. pancreas

Human Body 14 (p. 22)
1. excretory   2. kidney
3. bladder   4. skin
5. urethra

Human Body 15 (p. 22)
1. F 2. T 3. F 4. F 5. T

Human Body 16 (p. 23)
1. D 2. C 3. A 4. B

Human Body 17 (p. 23)
1. C 2. D 3. A 4. B

Human Body 18 (p. 23)
1. T 2. F 3. T 4. T 5. F

Human Body 19 (p. 23)
1. enamel   2. dentin
3. root   4. crown   5. gums

Human Body 20 (p. 24)
1. molars   2. incisors
3. deciduous   4. permanent
5. jaw

Human Body 21 (p. 24)
1. gene   2. chromosome
3. DNA   4. molecule
5. heredity

Human Body 22 (p. 24)
1. retina   2. lens   3. iris
4. pupil   5. cornea

Human Body 23 (p. 25)
1. bacteria   2. inoculation
3. virus   4. pathogen

Human Body 24 (p. 25)
1. B 2. A 3. D 4. C

Human Body 25 (p. 25)
1. fitness   2. flexibility
3. aerobic   4. endurance

Human Body 26 (p. 25)
1. C 2. A 3. E 4. B 5. D

Human Body 27 (p. 26)
1. A 2. E 3. C 4. B 5. D

Human Body 28 (p. 26)
1. balance   2. inner ear
3. semicircular canals 4. sensor

Human Body 29 (p. 26)
2. sweet   3. sour
4. salty   5. bitter
Listed foods will vary.

Human Body 30 (p. 26)
1. stimulus   2. pain
3. sensitive   4. irritation
5. dermis

Earth Science 1 (p. 27)
1. crust   2. inner core
3. mantle   4. outer core

Earth Science 2 (p. 27)
1. tectonics   2. continent
3. continental drift   4. plate

Earth Science 3 (p. 27)
1. fault   2. earthquake
3. wave   4. seismograph

Earth Science 4 (p. 27)
1. seismology, study of earthquakes
2. shallow, near the surface
3. tsunami, ocean wave caused by an earthquake
4. tremor, shaking
5. magnitude, size

Earth Science 5 (p. 28)
1. volcanic
2. ash
3. basalt
4. pumice
5. obsidian

Earth Science 6 (p. 28)
1. C 2. D 3. B 4. E 5. A

Earth Science 7 (p. 28)
1. toxic
2. explosive
3. solidify
4. eruption

Earth Science 8 (p. 28)
1. E 2. C 3. D 4. B 5. A

Earth Science 9 (p. 29)
1. seismometer
2. interior
3. exterior
4. epicenter
5. occur

Earth Science 10 (p. 29)
1. rock cycle
2. sedimentary
3. igneous
4. pressure
5. metamorphic

Earth Science 11 (p. 29)
1. marble
2. slate
3. granite
4. crystal
5. transform

Earth Science 12 (p. 30)
1. fossilization
2. hardened
3. skeletons
4. Impressions
5. shells

Earth Science 13 (p. 30)
1. stalactites
2. stalagmite
3. cavern
4. corrosive
5. dissolve

Earth Science 14 (p. 30)
1. Tides
2. gravity
3. bulge
4. spring
5. neap

Earth Science 15 (p. 31)
1. sandstone, sand
2. conglomerate; pebbles, sand, and clay
3. shale, clay
4. limestone, dissolved shells

Earth Science 16 (p. 31)
1. strata
2. erosion
3. weathering
4. conservation
5. resistant

Earth Science 17 (p. 31)
1. luster
2. hardness
3. color
4. streak color
5. crystal shape

Earth Science 18 (p. 31)
1. quartz
2. mineral
3. copper
4. pyrite
5. sulfur

Earth Science 19 (p. 32)
1. renewable resource, forests
2. nonrenewable resource, oil
3. alternative energy source, wind energy
4. pollution, smog

Earth Science 20 (p. 32)
1. anthracite
2. bituminous
3. fossils

Earth Science 21 (p. 32)
1. C 2. D 3. B 4. A

Earth Science 22 (p. 32)
1. uplifted
2. exposed
3. deposited
4. compressed

Earth Science 23 (p. 33)
1. A 2. C 3. B 4. D

Earth Science 24 (p. 33)
1. iceberg
2. retreating
3. advancing
4. valley
5. ice sheet

Earth Science 25 (p. 33)
1. coastal
2. arch
3. stack
4. undercutting

Earth Science 26 (p. 33)
1. D 2. A 3. E 4. B 5. C

Earth Science 27 (p. 34)
1. E 2. C 3. B 4. D 5. A

Earth Science 28 (p. 34)
1. current   2. depth
3. salinity   4. marine

Earth Science 29 (p. 34)
1. trenches   2. shallow
3. surface   4. island
5. hot spot

Earth Science 30 (p. 34)
1. mid-ocean   2. zone
3. sonar   4. sea floor
5. continent

Earth Science 31 (p. 35)
1. crevasse   2. compact
3. debris   4. boulders

Earth Science 32 (p. 35)
1. F 2. T 3. F 4. T 5. T

Earth Science 33 (p. 35)
1. any precious stone, gem
2. the hardest stone, diamond
3. fossilized tree sap, amber
4. a purple stone, amethyst
5. a green gem, emerald

Earth Science 34 (p. 35)
1. kelp   2. undersea
3. building up   4. breaking down

Atmos. & Space Science 1 (p. 36)
1. T 2. F 3. T 4. T 5. F

Atmos. & Space Science 2 (p. 36)
1. anemometer, wind speed
2. barometer, air pressure
3. hygrometer, humidity
4. thermometer, temperature
5. rain gauge, precipitation

Atmos. & Space Science 3 (p. 36)
1. asteroid   2. comet
3. meteor   4. meteorite

Atmos. & Space Science 4 (p. 36)
1. constellation   2. galaxy
3. star   4. black hole

Atmos. & Space Science 5 (p. 37)
1. drought   2. global warming
3. ozone   4. pollution
5. global

Atmos. & Space Science 6 (p. 37)
1. cosmologist   2. collapse
3. solar system   4. everything in space
5. hydrogen   6. helium

Atmos. & Space Science 7 (p. 37)
1. sunspots   2. flare
3. corona   4. eclipse
5. ultraviolet

Atmos. & Space Science 8 (p. 38)
1. inner planets   2. orbit
3. outer planets   4. planet

Atmos. & Space Science 9 (p. 38)
1. inner planets   2. rocky
3. Mercury   4. Venus
5. Earth   6. Mars

Atmos. & Space Science 10 (p. 38)
1. outer   2. gaseous
3. Jupiter   4. Saturn
5. Uranus   6. Neptune

Atmos. & Space Science 11 (p. 38)
1. Milky Way   2. telescope
3. cluster   4. local group
5. nebula

Atmos. & Space Science 12 (p. 39)
1. axis   2. gravity
3. rotation   4. revolution

Atmos. & Space Science 13 (p. 39)
1. D 2. C 3. A 4. B

Atmos. & Space Science 14 (p. 39)
1. barred   2. spiral
3. elliptical   4. collide

Atmos. & Space Science 15 (p. 39)
1. pulsar   2. red giant
3. supernova   4. quasar

Atmos. & Space Science 16 (p. 40)
1. D 2. A 3. B 4. E 5. C

Atmos. & Space Science 17 (p. 40)
1. dwarf   2. Kuiper belt
3. asteroid belt   4. impact
5. bodies

Atmos. & Space Science 18 (p. 40)
1. F 2. T 3. T 4. F 5. F

Atmos. & Space Science 19 (p. 40)
1. infrared   2. variations
3. carbon   4. circulate

Atmos. & Space Science 20 (p. 41)
1. El Niño   2. cold front
3. warm front   4. transpiration
5. evaporation

Atmos. & Space Science 21 (p. 41)
1. hurricane   2. tornado
3. thunderstorm   4. lightning
5. front   6. air mass

Atmos. & Space Science 22 (p. 42)
1. cirrus   2. cumulus
3. stratus   4. altocumulus
5. nimbus

Atmos. & Space Science 23 (p. 42)
1. precipitation   2. pattern
3. hail   4. snow
5. rain

Atmos. & Space Science 24 (p. 42)
1. F 2. T 3. T 4. T

Atmos. & Space Science 25 (p. 42)
1. C 2. A 3. D 4. E 5. B

Physical Science 1 (p. 43)
1. technology   2. fiber
3. metal   4. nonmetal
5. gold

Physical Science 2 (p. 43)
1. opaque   2. transparent
3. translucent   4. prism

Physical Science 3 (p. 43)
1. concave   2. convex
3. absorption   4. refraction
5. reflection

Physical Science 4 (p. 43)
1. enlarge, magnify
2. instrument to see faraway things, telescope
3. instrument to see very small things, microscope
4. instrument with two enlarging lenses, binoculars
5. glass curved to bend light, lens

Physical Science 5 (p. 44)
1. oscillate   2. amplitude
3. repetition   4. frequency

Physical Science 6 (p. 44)
1. metal   2. melted
3. nonmetal   4. metallurgist
5. alloy

Physical Science 7 (p. 44)
1., 2., 4., and 5. should be circled.

Physical Science 8 (p. 44)
1. acid   2. base   3. base
4. litmus 5. acid

Physical Science 9 (p. 45)
1. spectrum   2. infrared
3. ultraviolet   4. rainbow
5. optics

Physical Science 10 (p. 45)
1. F 2. T 3. F 4. T 5. F 6. F

Physical Science 11 (p. 45)
1. atom   2. molecule
3. element   4. periodic table
5. properties

Physical Science 12 (p. 46)
1. component   2. compound
3. mixture   4. solution
5. suspension

Physical Science 13 (p. 46)
1. gas   2. liquid   3. solid
4. melt   5. solidify

Physical Science 14 (p. 46)
1. attract   2. repel
3. compass   4. positive
5. negative

Physical Science 15 (p. 46)
1. B 2. A 3. D 4. C 5. E

Physical Science 16 (p. 47)
1. C 2. D 3. B 4. A

Physical Science 17 (p. 47)
1. circuit   2. breaker
3. insulator

Physical Science 18 (p. 47)
1. accelerate   2. decelerate
3. velocity   4. momentum

Physical Science 19 (p. 47)
1. kinetic　　2. stationary
3. conversion　4. potential

Physical Science 20 (p. 48)
1. energy　　2. fossil fuels
3. coal　　　4. petroleum
5. nonrenewable

Physical Science 21 (p. 48)
1. wheel and axle 2. ax
3. teeter-totter　4. ramp
5. scissors

Physical Science 22 (p. 49)
1. waste　　　2. destroyed
3. Heat　　　4. Hydroelectricity

Physical Science 23 (p. 49)
1. transfer energy 2. create
3. replaceable　4. supplemental

Physical Science 24 (p. 49)
1. geothermal　2. nuclear
3. wind (or wave) 4. solar
5. hydroelectric

Physical Science 25 (p. 49)
1. C 2. D 3. A 4. E 5. B

Science & Technology 1 (p. 50)
1. drag　　2. lift　　3. airfoil
4. weight　5. thrust

Science & Technology 2 (p. 50)
1. fission　　2. radioactive
3. uranium　4. neutron

Science & Technology 3 (p. 50)
1. grid　　　2. alternating
3. distribution　5. substation

Science & Technology 4 (p. 50)
1. C 2. A 3. E 4. B 5. D

Science & Technology 5 (p. 51)
1. F 2. T 3. T 4. F 5. T

Science & Technology 6 (p. 51)
1. phonographic 2. magnetic
3. digital　　4. laser

Science & Technology 7 (p. 51)
1. analog　　2. digital
3. bit　　　4. byte, bits

Science & Technology 8 (p. 51)
1. transistor　2. silicon
3. microprocessor 4. chip

Science & Technology 9 (p. 52)
1. T 2. F 3. F 4. F

Science & Technology 10 (p. 52)
1. information　2. database
3. network　　4. program

Science & Technology 11 (p. 52)
1. prototype　2. biometrics
3. miniaturization

Science & Technology 12 (p. 52)
1. cellulose　2. recycle
3. pulp　　　4. conveyor

Science & Technology 13 (p. 53)
1. E 2. A 3. B 4. D 5. C

Science & Technology 14 (p. 53)
1. transmitters　2. desalinization
3. conservation　4. pollution

Science & Technology 15 (p. 53)
1. T 2. F 3. F 4. T 5. T

Science & Technology 16 (p. 53)
1. genetic　　2. Pesticides
3. Biological

Science & Technology 17 (p. 54)
1. turbine　　2. reserves
3. harness　　4. windmills
5. wind farm

Science & Technology 18 (p. 54)
1. signal　　2. modem
3. code　　　4. electronic
5. decode

Science & Technology 19 (p. 54)
1. Copernicus　2. Galileo
3. Newton　　4. Mendel
5. Einstein